The Reality of Who We Are

Wilsee Kollie

BookLeaf
Publishing

India | USA | UK

Presentation by *BookLeaf Publishing*

Web: www.bookleafpub.com

E-mail: info@bookleafpub.com

ISBN: 9789360942946

First edition 2024

For my mommy–

You make me feel so loved because of your overflowing care. As much as you tell me I can do anything, I want to take this time to tell you that I know you can do anything you put your mind to. I love you, Mommy.

For my readers–

You are more than what you accomplish.

You don't have to figure it all out.

Take it day by day. You will be okay.

PREFACE

Back when I was younger, I had moments where I couldn't even look at myself. I had no emotion for the person who stared back at me in the mirror. When I did have emotions, it was only tears of sadness and exhaustion because when you hate yourself so deeply, the mirror isn't a friend but instead a reality check of everything you wish not to be.

You can only wish for…

I want a day of silence in my head
Of somber thoughts drifting away
I want a day of peace
Where I am no longer afraid

—-

I want a day of clarity
Where this misplacement of confusion no longer
exists
I want a day with no pain
Where things are no longer hard to bear

—-

I want a day where perfection is synonymous
with reality
I want a day of loving so deeply
where things can no longer shake me
I want a day of something that breaks the
pressures of consistency
I want a day of longevity

—

I strive for the feeling of floating freely
Where things can no longer hold me

Simultaneous.

2

Growing up was the hardest thing to do.
So many wounds. So many to cure.
Some were open, and some transparent.
Full of scars. Full of embarrassment.
—

But now I know,
they all tell stories.

—

Simultaneously broken and beautiful.

A reminder to you.

3

Stop looking at yourself like you aren't
beautiful.
You are meant to be in this world.
Don't dim your light just for somebody else.

You deserve the love that you give.
I need you to know that deep inside.

Stop looking at yourself like that.

You are meant to be in this world.
You are not a burden, you are enough.

I hear you.
I see you.
I understand you.

Let each version of you be a reflection of your
heart and not your body.

Faking (Pt. 1)

Pretty baby
creating false love.
Faking every second of
what really was.

Faking (Pt. 2)

I find myself acting.

And in my mind,
I create a world where I exist within a scene.
Only saying words that hold no meaning.

I say what I think they want me to say.
I do what I think they believe.

Faking (Pt. 3)

I feel like a fraud in my own body.
Scared to release any vulnerability,
because if I do,
they may break me.

But at the same time,
I do not fear that the most.

I think I am more scared that I will have no
emotion in the process,
when they break
the person who I act to be.

Invisible in spaces.

It is the words I say that make me feel so little.
It is the way I breathe.
It is the way I stutter when I say these words.
It is when I exhale.
It is when I inhale.

Holding my last breath in the conversation,
hoping someone responds
but all I hear is a clarity of silence.

But,
It is clarity I do not like.
I want a commotion.
I want one word over the other,
scrambling with excitement,
to say something back
to me.

But,
all I get is silence.

And,
that is why I have decided not to speak.
Instead, all I do is overthink.
That my words mean nothing,

but just air,
ready to go extinct.

Am I not worth listening to?
Do you not care for what I have to say?

Would it make a difference if I told you how it
takes all of me,
to share my thoughts out loud to the world,
because I know I might be ignored or shut
down?

Am I a broken record,
repeating just so you can hear me?

I am tired of my words just being thin air,
but I guess everyone has a role to play.
And by default, I'll be the listener in your show.

He loved me...

When he saw her, all he could do was observe
her for the beauty she held.
Every inch, from her coiled hair that bounced as
she moved with such delicacy.
Every inch, tracing her midnight skin with his
piercing eyes, the reason why he loved the stars.
Every inch, entering her mellow heart of
tenderness.

He didn't know why he loved this girl so much.
He just knew he couldn't.
But deep down, he needed her.

I love being a woman.

I am a divine soul.
My beauty is within.
I feel it,
rich in my skin.

I am a divine soul.
A being meant for more.

I am divinely feminine.

Growing and accepting all my identities.

In our beauty,
we have a connection.
That comes from in between our identities.

We share a blood so beautiful, so binding, and so
sane!

It's the beauty of my blackness and my culture,
that I share within my veins.

Keep busy.

13

Why do I always feel guilty for taking a break?
I rather overdose on tasks with no escape.

It feels like I'm running away,
from my fear of no mistakes.

To be perfect is to do,
every single day.
It's the only way,
for me not to feel like a fake.

Fear: A Haiku

Fear has the power,
to cloud us from seeing and
doing our purpose.

Silent body.

15

Silent body,
awaken from thee.
Show all my nakedness from beneath.
I was afraid to show you me,
just bare.

But that's all I want you to see.
That's all I want to share.

Rock bottom.

The differences we hold in ourselves,
are what we cannot hold in this world.
Society will not abide by this kind of health.

We keep our words,
until we burn them, too.
We hold our breaths,
until our heads turn blue.

Why not choose death,
and be made new.

Haiku #2

17

It takes the angry,
and the calm to start a fight,
a strong fight for change.

Life and Death

18

What does the idea of life have in common with
death?
It is a substance of shame and neglect.
We live our lives with no perception of what is
to be,
but we die not knowing what was before us.

Allowance

The substance of growing up.
It is a long journey.
As we all try to figure it out,
let us choose to be graceful to ourselves.

Allow yourself to start over.
Allow yourself to make a mistake.
Allow yourself to fail.

Attitude is Everything

Attitude is everything,
was the first mantra I ever learned.
To put a smile on my face,
and do my thang every single day.
And, as a black girl,
I did my thang.
I snatched that mantra and made it my bitch.

Because now,
every time I wake up,
I smile.
Every time I go for a stroll,
I smile.
Every time I speak my mind,
I smile.
And every time I wear my natural hair out,
you know for sure I smile.
And every time I disagree with what you say,
I smile, unfortunately.
And every time I feel emotions other than
happiness,
I smile.

And still,
I get called,

"The angry black girl."
—

Attitude is everything,
was the very first mantra I learned.

I learned that no matter how hard I tried to
sound as sweet as a button,

when I would say, "Hey can you please stop."
They would hear, "Do not mess with me."

When I would say, "I'm sorry."
They would hear, "What I got to be sorry
about?"

But really, what do I gotta be sorry about?
—

For most of my life,
as a black girl,
I have learned to play the part that society has
created.
Always obeying an unwritten rule to
"Stay put"
"Don't step out of bounds"
"Be 10x better"
Be this...
Be that...

But I just can't...
I can no longer breathe.

—

That's why I have made it my life journey to
scream out from the top of my lungs with all my
emotions,
with all my will.
Because it is my voice that guides me.
That makes me so real.

And as a black woman, my attitude is
everything!
The good,
and the bad,
and the in-between.
And if you can't handle all of that,
then…all I can say is, "Why don't you put a
smile on your face?"
And just let me be me.

Lost and found.

23

I was lost,
and I still am to this day.
Which is okay.

Remember,
create your journey,
and lead with faith.